When Friends Gather for Tea

Pouring Out Love with Tea and Kindness

Paintings and Text by

SANDY LYNAM CLOUGH

HARVEST HOUSE PUBLISHERS

EUGENE, OREGON

DEDICATION

This book is dedicated to these special ladies who were the first
to share the heart of Sandy's Tea Society with their own tea parties:

Pat Borysiewicz ✦ Ocee, Florida
LaNita Clark ✦ Highlands, North Carolina
Mary Cooper ✦ Eugene, Oregon
Ruth Ellen Polito ✦ Toms River, New Jersey
Sherrie Styles ✦ Titusville, Florida

My special thanks to Patti Brussat, Carol Ann Hickman, and Pat Borysiewicz
for sharing their teatime recipes with Sandy's Tea Society.

When Friends Gather for Tea
Copyright © 2002 by Sandy Lynam Clough
Published by Harvest House Publishers
Eugene, OR 97402

Library of Congress Cataloging-in-Publication Data
Clough, Sandy Lynam, 1948-
   When friends gather for tea / Sandy Lynam Clough.
      p. cm.
   ISBN 0-7369-0667-3 (hardcover : alk. paper)
   I. Title.
   TX736 .C68 2002
   641.5'3–dc21

                                    2001004683

Design and production by Koechel Peterson & Associates, Minneapolis, Minnesota

Printed in Hong Kong

02 03 04 05 06 07 08 09 10 11 /NG/ 10 9 8 7 6 5 4 3 2 1

Contents

On Sandy's Front Porch

WHAT A JOY IT IS TO FIND YOU HERE on my front porch! You must have seen the flag I put out announcing a Sandy's Tea Society party here today. Won't you stay and join us? Please settle yourself into one of these rocking chairs while I finish my last-minute preparations for this afternoon's tea, and I'll tell you all about Sandy's Tea Society before everyone else arrives.

The tea society is a unique group of friends who have developed very special friendships by delighting one another with creative ideas and a warmth of kindness at their tea parties. These six ladies open their hearts and homes and share with each other—  and with us—their original fashion styles, tea party themes, special recipes, and thoughtful acts of kindness. It is the tea society's dearest hope that their example of friendship will encourage other ladies to join together to take tea and to build true friendships.

This group of ladies honored me by naming their group Sandy's Tea Society, for I was the one who introduced them and suggested that they have tea together. You'll see right away that they are kindred hearts and possibly very much like you. The Sandy's Tea Society motto is "Joining Kindred Hearts with a Cup of Friendship," and a tea party is the perfect place to do that. I'll let the ladies introduce themselves to you when they arrive. They've been invited here today so I can surprise them with a new friendship idea that might inspire you as well!

Now, I'll just place this platter of cookies on my favorite embroidered cloth topping the tea table, and it looks like I'm just in time. Do you hear the welcome sound of cheerful chatting? Let's wave at the ladies as they hurry up the walk, and please join me in giving each of them a fond welcome as they come up the porch steps.

I'm so delighted to see my tea society friends looking about at the porch swing draped with a pretty wedding ring quilt, the flower garden quilt on the wicker settee, and the collection of rocking chairs. That's Gloria who is clapping her hands in delight. And all the ladies are smiling broadly. See them rush to try out the rocking chairs—yes, they realize we're having a front porch tea party!

The first time these ladies came to tea at my home, they didn't know each other at all. Today, they are such good friends that I've asked them to introduce each other to you.

Lillian speaks up quickly. "Ruby is an artist with a creative mind like quicksilver and a heart of gold. She is usually as short on time as she is long on ideas, but we always count on her colorful personality to sprinkle our time together with a little fun!"

Suzette does not hesitate to add, "Gloria is an outdoor girl. She loves a good game of croquet and long nature walks. She is also a bride-to-be, and I wouldn't be surprised if this dear young lady is planning a garden wedding at sunset."

"Lillian's gentle spirit is like a rose without thorns," Laura volunteers. "She adores the romance of roses and decorates everything with roses and rose patterns. Not only is she a very good seamstress, she's always ready to help someone else who can't sew a stitch."

Claudette shares, "Laura is quiet and elegant, as you can see, and a mother-to-be—as you can also see! We're all excited about helping her and her husband welcome their first child into the world. Books are so special to Laura that I wouldn't be surprised if she were already reading aloud to this precious, unborn baby."

Ruby presents tenderhearted Claudette. "She collects well-loved old things like vintage teacups and antique silver and lace. She doesn't look for perfection in antiques or friends, but instead looks for the character that the chips and cracks of life impart."

"Suzette's name is almost synonymous with 'cottage garden,'" Gloria says. "Her countenance is as refreshing as the daisies she grows, and her home is as rich and cheerful in color as the vintage printed hankies she collects."

Ruby has brought her new neighbor, Veronica, to our group. This lovely lady is very stylish, yet comfortably unassuming. Although her husband's business has caused their family to move frequently, her warmth and friendliness help her to fit in very quickly.

Suzette's mother, Claire, has recently moved in with Suzette and her family, and she has joined us for the first time today. She has a winsome personality and so many creative skills we would all like to learn. We wouldn't be surprised at all if she started a "Silver Tea Society" as soon as she meets some ladies her age here.

What a charming and gracious group of friends!

As I begin to pour the tea, Gloria remarks,

"What a delightful idea to have a tea party on the porch! What made you think of it?"

"Actually, I frequently sit out here to enjoy my tea," I reply. "I think of it as a peaceful island between the chores inside and the errands outside."

"Oh, look! The cake is decorated with patchwork squares like a quilt!" points out Suzette, as I cut a square of cake for each lady.

"And the cookies are square, too, and iced like gingham, striped, or dotted fabric," adds Claudette.

"You usually surround yourself with so much lace and vintage china for an elegant tea that I am a little surprised that you decorated the porch for our party with quilts," notes Laura.

"I especially wanted this tea to have a warm and comfortable feeling since we have new friends here for the first time," I explain. "Besides, this group is like a beautiful quilt that is being pieced together. Every square is different, but harmonious. And like a soft, old quilt,

good friends are both comfortable and useful."

"If this group were a quilt, it would definitely be a 'friendship quilt!'" declares Ruby.

"Actually, the quilt that is covering our tea table *is* a friendship quilt that Claire pulled out of her trunk for me."

"You mean people actually made friendship quilts?" asks Gloria. "Is that why there are names on the quilt?"

"Yes, indeed. It was traditional for each lady to embroider her name—and possibly the date—on a block," I answer. "The whole quilt together made a wonderful remembrance of friendship and happy hours spent together."

Claudette turns to Claire. "Would you please tell us about your friendship quilt?"

"Well," Claire replies, "I didn't have a part in making it. It was my mother's, and it was made by all the ladies who used to gather at our house regularly for quilting bees when I was a little girl."

"Was quilting the main thing you remember your mother and her friends doing together? Did they quilt instead of having tea parties like ours?" wonders Gloria.

"Oh, no. They met together for tea, too, and planned ways to help and befriend their neighbors, as well as each other," Claire remembers.

"I wish they had embroidered their acts of kindness on this quilt and left us a record of the things that they did to give us some ideas," Claudette says thoughtfully as she moves her fingers softly across an embroidered signature. "Wouldn't it be wonderful if we could continue their legacy of helping hands and hearts?"

"Why don't we do what they didn't do!" exclaims Ruby. We could see that her mind was racing.

"What do you mean?" puzzles Gloria.

"Why don't we begin using our tea parties as helping hands and helping hearts for our friends and neighbors," Ruby begins to explain, "and..."

"Yes!" Lillian had caught the vision. "And together we can make a friendship quilt with blocks that illustrate our acts of kindness for others!"

"Exactly!" agrees Ruby.

"And we can pass it down to the next generation to encourage them to show love to others," adds Laura.

Now everyone was excited!

"There is only one problem," cautions Gloria. "Some of us don't sew and don't know how to make a quilt block—much less a quilt!"

"Don't worry," Claire speaks up. "I have plenty of spare time to give instructions to anyone who needs help. Lillian and Ruby both sew. They can help as well. I think your idea is a splendid one!"

"I'll give it my best," promises Gloria. "I only hope that my crooked stitches won't spoil the project."

"They can't," Ruby assures her. "If you do it with your heart, it will be beautiful."

Suddenly Suzette remembers my promise to them. "Is this our surprise?"

"No, actually your surprise is under the cushion of your chair."

The air fills with tinkling and clinking sounds as the ladies stand up and look for a safe resting place for their teacups before they reach under the cushions in their rocking chairs. All of them retrieve identical packages.

Ruby unwraps hers first and reveals a lovely, embroidered apron with a card that simply says, "Serving one another in love."

"Is this from you?" she asks me.

"It might be from a Secret Sipper," I say mysteriously.

Laura looks up from her pretty apron. "You mean a Secret Sister?"

"No, a Secret Sipper is a teatime friend who secretly looks for little ways to help and bless you between teatimes—when you least expect it!"

"Do we all have a Secret Sipper friend?" wonders Claudette as the ladies look from one to the other.

"You will after today. Taped to the bottom of your saucer is the name of your Secret Sipper, who is one of this group."

Ruby covers her saucer with her napkin and then peeks under it. She smiles, her eyes twinkling. Following Ruby's lead, each lady in turn finds a way to shield her saucer or turn away to see this special name.

"What fun this will be! We can truly do something kind for someone without expecting anything in return!" cheers Claudette.

"As you focus on your teas for others for your friendship quilt, Secret Sippers will help you to not neglect your own friendships," I assure them.

"I would love to have the first tea!" Suzette turns to Veronica. "Please be our honored guest at a 'Welcome, New Neighbor' tea—just for you."

"I would be delighted!" says Veronica with a grateful smile.

I invite you to sit a little deeper in a cozy rocking chair with a warm cup of tea and join us for these special tea parties where Sandy's Tea Society uses teapots to pour out love as well as warm friendship.

A "Welcome, New Neighbor" Tea

SUZETTE AWOKE TO A SOFT TINKLING sound coming through her open window and sat up in bed with a start. "I've slept through my tea party! They've started without me!" Not fully awake, she bounded from her bed and looked out the window. What a relief! It was just barely dawn, not nearly time for the party to begin. Groggy, but too intrigued by the musical sound that had awakened her to go back to sleep, Suzette tripped down the back stairs and gingerly picked a barefoot path through the garden before she stopped. There hanging from the lowest branch of her apple tree was a beautiful wind chime. It was like having a music box in her garden!

Walking back to the house smiling, she wondered, "Who could have?" Ah! Her mother!

"Mother!" she called as she walked into the kitchen. "Thank you for the lovely wind chimes. What a nice addition they make to the garden!"

Claire looked up as she poured her morning coffee. "Oh, I didn't do that, dear."

Glancing up at the stairs, Suzette called for her husband, Paul. Without looking up, her mother commented, "It wasn't him either."

Veronica's Hat

"Then," Suzette asked, "who?"

"I have no idea," Claire replied with raised eyebrows, suppressing a grin. "Sounds like a Secret Sipper to me."

Suzette had planned a four o'clock outdoor garden tea to properly welcome Veronica to the tea society. As she had thought of all the places that Veronica had lived—Florida, California, Texas, Canada—Suzette was especially grateful for her own cottage and her pretty garden. She liked being planted in one place where she was able to watch the roses inch across the arbor and the apple tree spread year by year.

When planning the tea party, Suzette realized that if Veronica had a garden or any plants at her last home, she'd probably had to leave them behind when she was uprooted. This had given Suzette an idea! She created her tea invitations (for everyone except Veronica) on plain white cards on which she attached a single pressed pansy and wrote this request:

Please join us as we say,
You're as welcome as flowers in May.
Veronica is the one we greet.

Your presence will make it complete!
Tea is in the garden (unless it showers).
Please wear a dress all covered in flowers.
Alas, but her new garden is bare,
Let's show her that our tea society cares!
A plant from each of us will "wow" her
As we shower her with flowers!

As she slid each invitation into its envelope, Suzette sprinkled dried, fragrant rose petals inside before she sealed it. And right before she mailed the invitations, she had sprayed the envelopes with a lovely floral perfume.

Suzette had "dead headed" and watered her flowers early in the day and pulled her table into the center of the garden. Now it was almost teatime, and things were looking very festive for this "Welcome, New Neighbor" tea.

The creaking of the garden gate alerted Suzette that Veronica had arrived. As she welcomed her warmly, Veronica couldn't wait to thank Suzette. "I am so grateful not only for the generosity of your hospitality, but also for your offer of friendship. I hope the fragrance of this tea will often remind you of my gratitude." She handed Suzette a small basket filled with teas that were flavored with herbs and flowers such as rose petal, chamomile, and lemon verbena—a fragrant bouquet in itself.

As the other tea society members arrived, each lady in turn presented Veronica with a potted plant. All of them had chosen a vintage container—a teapot without a lid, a watering can, a ceramic planter—that Veronica could take with her if she had to move again.

Then Ruby discovered something. In mock horror, she put her hands to her face, gasping and pointing to the table.

"What, what?" asked Gloria as they rushed to the table.

"Bugs!" Ruby declared with a giggle. Bugs on the table were certainly a tea society first! But they all laughed in delight when they reached the table and saw these. Here and there across the white tablecloth Suzette had fastened jeweled pins of bees, ladybugs, dragonflies, and butterflies that she had either collected herself or borrowed from her mother's jewelry box.

Laughing at her friends' reaction, Suzette asked Claire to please pour the strawberry tea as she served her delectable treats—"bumblebees," shortbread cookies cut into butterfly shapes and decorated with icing and sprinkles, ladybug scones, and tropical chicken salad sandwiches.

SUZETTE'S TEA TABLE

❧ On the back of each chair, Suzette hung an inexpensive, wide-brimmed straw hat to which she had added a simple black ribbon for the ladies to wear and then take home. Parked close by was her antique wicker tea cart—ready to display the plants Veronica would receive from her new friends. Already a pot of Suzette's sunny daisies, complete with planting instructions, beamed a welcome from the bottom shelf.

❧ Knowing that the ladies themselves in their floral dresses would create a bright bouquet of color, Suzette chose a plain white tablecloth for her tea table. In the center she placed a child's little wooden wheelbarrow filled with potted geraniums and cascading petunias and ivy. By raiding her own cupboard of vintage china and borrowing here and there, Suzette was able to set the table with vintage floral china, making sure that not one piece matched—a veritable china garden!

❧ Beside each plate she displayed a brand-new pair of cotton print garden gloves, into which she tucked the silverware. In the center of each plate she set a brand-new little flowerpot filled with chocolate mousse and topped with chocolate shavings (to look like dirt) with a perky silk flower glued to a wooden stick displayed in the middle.

As a way of helping Veronica get better acquainted with the tea society, Suzette initiated the conversation by asking each lady to share about the best part of a place in which she had lived. She also asked them to recall any unusual experiences they had had while moving.

After a few good laughs over moving mishaps that were much funnier now than when they actually happened, the conversation turned to special people in faraway places who had planted joy, comfort, or companionship in their lives. A few eyes glistened with tears as they described friendships that miles could not separate and time could not end.

"I think that all of us," commented Lillian, "have found kindred hearts that have offered warm friendship in every kind of location. Home truly is where the heart is."

"Other times when I have left my home and my old friends behind for a brand-new place," confided Veronica, "like a ladybug, I have wanted to fly away back home. But your welcome has made me feel very much at home here already."

"Remember the verse that describes our friendship," reminded Claudette. " 'Make new friends, but keep the old. These are silver, those are gold.' Silver friends are as much a treasure as golden friends," she assured Veronica as she handed her a final gift. It was a map of their town

Susette's Teacup

with the way to each of their homes marked as well as the location of several churches she might like to visit and all of their favorite stores.

"Claire, you are also our beautiful new silver friend," continued Claudette, "and I am planning a tea for you that will showcase your beautiful handwork and honor those special skills that those with silver hair can share. Few of us know how to tat, embroider, crochet, or make lace! I hope that you will bring some of the beautiful things you have made to show us."

"Claire has already been teaching me how to applique so that I can stitch my quilt block," interjected Gloria. "Her willingness to help me and her patience have caused me to reflect on the debt of gratitude I have to all my teachers. If Claudette is going to honor Claire at a tea, I would like to host another sort of tea— a 'Thank You, Teacher' tea. Would you all help me? I'm ready to start learning how to cook."

Laura spoke for them all. "We'll be there!"

"Welcome, New Neighbor"

TEA MENU

Tropical Chicken Salad Sandwiches
Bumblebees
Shortbread Cookies
Ladybug Scones
Strawberry Tea

TROPICAL CHICKEN SALAD SANDWICHES

4 cooked chicken breasts—roasted or poached, then diced

2 tablespoons fresh lime juice

2 cups mango, cubed (2 fresh, ripe mangoes)

2 cups papaya, cubed (1 large, ripe, seeded papaya)

2 cups celery, chopped

4 scallions, chopped (both green and white part)

¼ cup nonfat plain yogurt

¼ cup lowfat mayonnaise ✦ 1 teaspoon curry powder

1 teaspoon ground cumin ✦ mixed green lettuce leaves

Mix together chicken breasts, lime juice, mango, papaya, celery, and scallions. Whisk together the yogurt, mayonnaise, curry powder, and cumin to make the salad dressing. Pour dressing over fruit and chicken mix. Place salad on a bed of mixed green lettuce leaves when ready to serve.

BUMBLEBEES

1 cup creamy peanut butter ✦ ½ cup powdered milk ✦ ½ cup graham cracker crumbs

1 teaspoon cinnamon ✦ 1 tablespoon honey ✦ slivered almonds

1 tube of chocolate icing (with fine point)

Mix all ingredients together except for chocolate icing and slivered almonds. Add more graham crackers or honey, if necessary, to achieve a consistency for molding. Form into little logs for the bodies. Add 2 slivered almonds for the wings. Use chocolate tube icing (with fine point) for the stripes and eyes. Place on a plate lined with unsprayed and washed fern fronds or other leaves. A few Shasta daisies or black-eyed Susans are a nice touch!

LADYBUG SCONES

2 cups flour ✦ 2 teaspoons baking powder

1 tablespoon sugar ✦ ½ teaspoon salt

4 tablespoons butter (real) ✦ 2 eggs, beaten

½ cup cream (half-and-half can be used, but the flavor won't be as rich)

½ cup dried cranberries, diced

Preheat oven to 425 degrees. Lightly butter a cookie sheet and set aside. In a large mixing bowl, mix flour, baking powder, sugar, and salt. Cut in butter until mixed well and coarse crumbs form. Add beaten eggs and cream until well blended (but don't beat or mix for too long). Add dried cranberry bits. Turn onto a lightly floured board and, with floured hands, knead dough for about a minute, being careful not to over-knead. Roll dough ¾-inch thick and cut out with a round cookie cutter. Place on a cookie sheet and bake for 15 minutes or until lightly browned. Cool for a couple of minutes on a cookie sheet before transferring to cooling racks.

SHORTBREAD COOKIES

1 cup butter, softened ✦ 1 cup powdered sugar

2 ½ cups all-purpose flour ✦ 2 tablespoons water

¾ teaspoon flavored extract (almond is a favorite, but vanilla and peppermint are wonderful as well)

¼ teaspoon salt

Combine butter and sugar in a large mixing bowl. Beat with a mixer on medium or by hand until creamy (about 2 minutes). Slowly add flour, water, extract, and salt; mixing well until thoroughly blended (about 2-3 minutes). Cover mixture and refrigerate until firm (about 1 hour). Preheat oven to 325 degrees. Roll chilled dough on flour-covered surface, one-half batch at a time (keeping remaining dough refrigerated) to about ½-inch thickness. Cut with a 2- or 3-inch cookie cutter. (Suzette cut her cookies into butterfly shapes.) Place cookies on ungreased cookie sheet and bake for 15-20 minutes, until just lightly browned on the edges. Remove from oven and cool completely. When cool, cookies can be decorated with frosting, sprinkles, and candies.

A "Thank You, Teacher" Tea

"THE MOST CURIOUS THING HAPPENED to me this morning," said Laura to the rest of the tea society as they prepared the food for Gloria's tea. "Now that it's very obvious I'm expecting, it's getting harder to bend over or stoop down to weed my flower beds. I thought that I just might have to give up on them until after the baby comes. But this morning when I stepped outside, I found them perfectly weeded!"

The ladies looked around mysteriously at one another and in unison said with glee, "A Secret Sipper!" Without revealing anything more, they went back to their cooking.

As Laura measured the flour, she stole a glance at their bride-to-be. The light caught a tear rolling down Gloria's cheek.

"Gloria," Laura said gently, "those are apples you're chopping—not onions. Is there something wrong?"

"Only everything," Gloria lamented. "My fiancé wanted to have the wedding inside and I wanted to have it outside. I insisted on my way, and now I'm afraid that I have ruined everything!

Sandy Lynam Clough

We haven't spoken in several days. I'm so sorry that I acted so selfishly. What if it's too late to apologize?"

Laura gave Gloria a little hug and Lillian assured her that in all her born days she had never seen a wedding without at least one party upset, but she had seen many happy marriages. Gloria brightened at their optimism and purposed to apologize as soon as the tea was over. Just the prospect of righting her wrong cheered her countenance.

In fact, giggles and laughter soon replaced her tears. Ruby started it by sharing one wedding catastrophe. She had seen a bride who had lost her slip going down the aisle and, without even glancing down, had paused, stepped out of it, kicked it aside, and continued down the aisle as if nothing had happened!

Suzette joined in with a story of her own. "Did you hear about the poor groom whose friends had painted a message on the bottom of his shoes? When he knelt at the altar with his bride, his shoes spelled out an SOS—'Help Me!'"

This started a flow of stories about how perfection rarely happens in the emotionally charged atmosphere of a wedding. There was the florist who brought the wrong flowers, the cake that was dropped on the way to the church, the invitations that were never delivered, the five hundred people who showed up at a reception for three hundred, and the mother-in-law who wore black!

Hearing those stories gave Gloria a new perspective on her own situation. Fixing her own problem now seemed so easy! Although no one had mentioned thunderstorms, her fiancé's preference for an indoor wedding was looking wiser all the time. Now she could truly enjoy preparing for this tea party she had planned so well.

It had been great fun for Gloria to think up what she would serve. Apples for a teacher seemed to be the perfect menu item. Every recipe had apples in it. Gloria had borrowed cups and saucers and dessert plates with apples on them, but since the group was so large for this tea, she used the apple china to designate a teacher "guest" place. In between, she used Laura's white china for the tea society ladies, who were all wearing plaid dresses or skirts for a "back to school" look.

Eager to get a gold star in promptness, the ladies scurried to place the apple-for-teacher tea sandwiches, apple dip, fruit salad sandwiches, and apple-apricot bread on the table before the doorbell rang. At the very last minute, Gloria placed apples at each place with a horizontal slit in the top into which she placed a placard.

Ding! Dong! Letting Gloria lead the way, the tea society ladies went as a group to answer the doorbell. They all had a special guest to welcome, for each of them had invited a teacher. Their guests were old and young, silver and golden teachers who had joyfully shared the treasures from their minds and hearts with room-fuls of young charges.

As they gathered around the table, Gloria gave each of the tea society ladies an oppor-tunity to introduce herself and her guest before the apple-cinnamon tea was poured. And after everyone was served, the ladies each shared a memory or story illustrating why her teacher was so special and memorable in her life. Then she presented her teacher with an A+ report card to express thanks for her caring qualities.

What happy times the ladies began to recall as they mingled their memories of bygone school days! Ruby reminisced with admiration about her elementary school teachers. "Imagine teaching second and third graders how to weave colored strands of crepe paper around a maypole in the spring, and then preparing children for a musical at Christmas in addition to teaching reading, geography, math, and history."

"I remember what perfect ladies my teachers

GLORIA'S BACK-TO-SCHOOL TABLE

❧ With Claire's help, Gloria made a long tablecloth out of a "back-to-school" cotton plaid fabric and plaid napkins. She topped the table on the diagonal with a smaller square cloth that looked like a chalkboard. To make the "chalkboard," Gloria started with a 36-inch square of black fabric to which she added a 2-inch wide border of brown fabric around the edge. Using white fabric paint in a squeezable bottle, she neatly printed alphabet letters and numbers randomly across the cloth.

❧ To serve her teatime goodies, Gloria made very unique containers. At the thrift store, she found several large and medium sized books of no real literary importance. She purchased them and, using a utility knife, very carefully cut the center out of the pages, leaving a large square hole with both of the covers still intact. She positioned each book with the cover open and a fresh square of plaid fabric displayed diagonally on the hole. She served the sandwiches in the books! Gloria also stacked extra books under some to vary the height. In the middle of the table she placed a random stack of books with a small world globe perched on top.

were. I admired them so in their suits and tailored dresses and sensible heels as they stood at the blackboard. But they weren't too proper to take us out to recess, or to push back the desks and teach us the Virginia reel on rainy days!" remembered Claudette.

"Don't forget square dancing!" added Lillian.

"I so appreciate the love of reading I received from my teachers. There was a certain security, too, in the order they gave to our little lives. My teacher started the day with a verse of Scripture and the pledge of allegiance to the flag. Although we liked to giggle and whisper when the teacher was out of the room, we knew to straighten up when we heard the click-click-click of her heels coming down the hall," Laura shared.

"I'll never forget the teacher who chose me, a little girl, to be Uncle Sam in the class play because she thought I would do the best job. And she didn't ask me to dress like a boy, either!" laughed Suzette.

"Do you remember," asked Ruby, "what a delicious secret it was to know your teacher's first name?"

All too soon, the chiming of the mantel

Gloria's Teacup

clock brought them back from their scholastic journey, and it was time to say their good-byes. Since Gloria's guest had traveled a bit of a distance, the other tea society ladies insisted on doing the cleanup so that Gloria could extend her visit with her teacher.

As they put away the last clean dish, Lillian turned to Claudette. "You know that our friend Diana has not been well. I talked to her last week and found that her doctor has prescribed bed rest for her. She so misses being active. Why don't we all take her a 'Wishing You Well' tea party?"

"Oh, let's do! Hopefully our little tea party will be a cup of encouragement for her."

After Gloria had waved good-bye to her favorite teacher, she found that the tea society had left her kitchen sparkling clean and had slipped out the back door. The street lamps came on just as she closed her front door behind her and stepped outside into the night air. Her mind was so set on her peace-seeking mission with her fiancé that she almost tripped over a lovely white basket lined with a small tablecloth that had been secretly left on her front porch. Peeking inside, she found a candle, two roses in a little vase, two teacups and saucers, some of the leftover tea time treats from their party, and a carafe of hot tea.

A little note attached to the handle read, "Humili-tea is irresistible!" Armed with everything she needed for a romantic tea for two, Gloria was indeed a bride-to-be on a mission!

"Thank You, Teacher"
TEA MENU

Apple-for-Teacher Tea Sandwiches
Apple Dip
Fruit Salad Sandwiches
Apple-Apricot Bread
Apple-Cinnamon Tea

APPLE-FOR-TEACHER
TEA SANDWICHES

2 cups chicken breast, diced

¾ cup mayonnaise (1 cup if needed for moistness)

½ cup curry powder ✦ ½ teaspoon mango chutney

½ teaspoon lemon juice ✦ ¼ cup canned water chestnuts, diced

½ cup sliced almonds ✦ ¼ cup celery, diced

1 cup apples, finely diced ✦ ½ cup flaked coconut

1 loaf of your favorite bread, sliced

organically grown pansies ✦ circular cookie cutter

Combine chicken breast, mayonnaise, curry powder, chutney, and lemon juice in a bowl. Add water chestnuts, celery, almonds, coconut, and apples. Mix thoroughly. Spread a thick layer of salad onto a slice of bread. Cut out circle shape using cookie cutter or cut into four squares or triangles with a knife. Garnish with a pansy.

APPLE DIP

8 ounces cream cheese (room temperature)

¾ cup brown sugar

¼ cup sugar ✦ 1 teaspoon vanilla

*slices of fruit or whole fruits of your choice—
sliced apples, sliced pears, whole strawberries, etc.*

Whip all ingredients together until blended and smooth. Cover and let sit in refrigerator for 2 hours. Serve dip in a small bowl and surround with fruit.

FRUIT SALAD SANDWICHES

1 ½ cups mild cheddar cheese, finely grated

½ cup dates, chopped

½ cup pecans

½ cup mayonnaise

3 large apples, peeled and cored

1 large can pineapple slices, drained

lemon juice

Combine cheese, dates, pecans, and mayonnaise in food processor and blend until smooth. If you do not have a food processor, be sure to finely chop the dates and pecans. Slice apples into ¼-inch thick rings, then sprinkle with lemon juice to keep from turning brown. Make your sandwiches using an apple slice for the bottom, a layer of mayonnaise mixture for the middle, and a pineapple slice for the top.

APPLE-APRICOT BREAD

⅔ cup boiling water

1 cup apricots, diced ✦ 2 cups white flour

2 ½ teaspoons baking powder

¼ teaspoon baking soda ✦ ½ teaspoon salt

½ teaspoon allspice

½ teaspoon cinnamon

milk (see directions)

½ cup shortening ✦ ¾ cup sugar

1 egg, beaten ✦ 1 cup apple, chopped

¾ cup walnuts, chopped

Pour boiling water over apricots and let stand for 15 minutes. Remove apricots from water and add milk to the water to make ⅔ cup in all. Sift together flour, baking powder, soda, salt, allspice and cinnamon. Cream together the sugar and shortening. Beat in the egg. Add dry ingredients alternately with the liquid. Fold in the fruit and walnuts. Spoon into a greased and floured 9- x 5-inch pan. Bake in a preheated 350-degree oven for 1 hour. Cool on rack.

A "Wishing You Well" Tea

"I DON'T KNOW WHICH IS WORSE," sympathized Lillian as she and Claudette walked home from their friend Diana's house. "Having to endure dirty hair or a dusty house when you are sick."

"That's easy. Dirty hair," sighed Claudette. They were both tired but deeply satisfied that their friend had both clean hair and a clean house. Their "Wishing You Well" tea party was tomorrow. The tea society had planned it with Diana's husband, Steven, to be a surprise for her. Knowing that Diana would want to look her best and have her house look nice, Claudette and Lillian had spent the day cleaning house, doing Diana's hair and nails, and even preparing dinner and

Sandy Lynam Clough

popping it in the oven. Their friend had no idea that there was another surprise to come.

Nor did Lillian and Claudette! When each of them arrived at home, they found that someone had cleaned their house and left a casserole in the oven for them, too. What blessings Secret Sippers are!

∽

At ten o'clock the next morning, Diana's husband looked out the front window and saw a sight that both made him laugh and warmed his heart. Coming down the front walk with baskets and hatboxes full of goodies were all the ladies in Sandy's Tea Society—dressed in their bathrobes and slippers, coming to cheer his sick wife! As funny as they looked, he was deeply grateful for their sensitivity. Diana would not be the only one who was not decked out in a teatime frock.

The tea party was timed so that Steven could take care of some errands during this "girlfriend" visit. He escorted Lillian and Claudette to Diana's room and said good-bye to his sweet wife, whose spirits were already buoyed by this unexpected visit. While the other ladies readied the tea table, Lillian and Claudette helped Diana get up, smooth her hair, and put on her robe and slippers.

"Oh," said Diana, "I feel like a queen in this robe! Imagine a tea party just for me."

"And I almost forgot your 'crown,'" laughed Claudette, producing a pretty hat with pastel flowers.

As she entered her living room, Diana was met with hugs all around and seated in a chair of honor to witness a most unique fashion show. Wearing her prettiest teatime hat, each of the ladies modeled her bathrobe. Ruby gave the commentary, beginning with Gloria: "And here we have Gloria modeling a vintage plaid flannel robe in shades of green, purple, and brown— perfectly toned for hiding behind the neighbor's bushes so the milkman won't see her chasing her dog down the street. Note how the collar turns up, partially concealing her identity. This delightful blend of beauty and practicality is also warm enough for the crisp morning air." Gloria modeled with aplomb, performing quarter turns in her hat laden with wax fruit and giving "beauty queen" waves to her audience.

Next was Lillian, described by Ruby as so well camouflaged in her rose-print robe that her husband lost her for three days in their rose-papered kitchen! By the time Suzette modeled her patchwork robe, they were all weak with laughter.

As the ladies gathered around the table for tea, Diana was amazed to see that even the table wore a robe! Lillian had made a tablecloth out of a chenille bedspread that was white with pastel flowers. By looking through their own cabinets and visiting a few thrift shops, Lillian and Claudette had found teacups, saucers, dessert plates, and a teapot in several solid, pastel colors. Lillian had hemmed napkins from pink and white, yellow and white, and blue and white polka dot fabrics and then trimmed them in white rick-rack. The effect was so fresh and feminine!

Since Diana was eating a careful diet,

healthful tea treats had been carefully chosen—fresh fruit, cheesecake cupcakes, coconut dream bars, vegetable sandwiches, and carob buttermilk cake. The tea society ladies were careful as they sipped their orange spice tea not to chatter on about life "on the outside" and all the activities that Diana was missing. Instead, they wished to listen to her—her hopes, her fears, and the patterns of her days. Soon it was time to tuck Diana back into bed before she became too tired.

Leaving her with the encouragement of their continued care, the tea society placed a stack of pretty hatboxes by her bed. In the largest were three books and some vintage beads and gloves.

"I will come visit you once a week and read from this historical novel," promised Laura, lifting a romantic favorite from the box. "And we shall wear our hats and gloves and pearls while we read, and pass the tissue box back and forth until our heroine finds her true love."

Claudette picked up the next box. "In this cookbook are my favorite recipes. Each of them is marked with the date that I'm bringing you that dish for dinner."

Ruby produced a book and several old-fashioned pens from a smaller box. "This journal is totally blank. In it you can write and draw your dreams and your days. If you record your path

GLORIA'S "POST OFFICE" BOX

Choose a few basics—cards, envelopes, postage stamps—and several goodies—fun pens, stickers, confetti—for a fun and thoughtful gift.

❊ assortment of cards and envelopes—birthday, thank you, anniversary, blank, etc.

❊ pretty note paper

❊ colored and "fun" pens—jelly, milky, glitter, scented, etc.

❊ postage stamps

❊ return address labels or personalized address stamp

❊ stickers

❊ rubber stamps

❊ rubber stamp pads in assorted colors

❊ lettering template

❊ confetti

❊ decorative paper punches

❊ small book of poems or quotations

Lillian's Teacup

through this season of your life, your journey may be an encouragement to others."

"In the striped box," Lillian said, "is a counted cross-stitch project with all of the supplies you need to work on it."

"The next box is a 'post office box,'" pointed out Gloria. "Inside are note cards, pens, and stamps to help you stay in touch with friends and family."

"And the box on top is a 'box of blessings,'" shared Suzette. "I've filled it with Scriptures, quotes, and words of comfort and encouragement to brighten your days."

"They are *all* boxes of blessings!" exclaimed Diana. "I am so deeply grateful to all of you. I do not have enough words to express it. My mother was so right—a friend in need is a friend indeed!"

∽

"Did visiting Diana make you sad?" Ruby asked Laura later as she walked home from the tea party with her quieter-than-normal friend.

"Oh, no," protested Laura. "Diana encouraged me. She has demonstrated to me that it is possible to live through a difficult time with

grace, patience, and hope. It is my own doubts that are making me sad. The closer I come to the birth of my baby, the more I realize how little I know about being a mother. I wish my own mother lived nearby. There are so many things I would like to know about mothering before I am one. I need some instructions!"

"Can she not come for a visit?" ventured Ruby.

"She is coming after the baby is born. I'm afraid that in all the excitement, even then I will never find out all the things about being a mother that are really important. What I truly want is a mother's heart!"

As Laura confided her feelings, it occurred to Ruby that what might help Laura most was not necessarily a mother's point of view, but rather a child's point of view. She tried to keep up her end of the conversation the rest of the way home, but already her mind was racing with plans for a "Heart of a Mother" tea for this mother-to-be.

"Wishing You Well"

TEA MENU

Cheesecake Cupcakes
Coconut Dream Bars
Vegetable Sandwiches
Carob Buttermilk Cake
Fresh Fruit
Orange Spice Tea

CHEESECAKE CUPCAKES

3 eight-ounce packages of cream cheese (room temperature)

5 eggs

⅔ cup honey

½ teaspoon vanilla

Beat cream cheese (at room temperature) until fluffy. Add other ingredients and beat. Pour into paper-lined muffin tins. Bake at 300 degrees for 40 minutes. Cool for 5 minutes.

Filling:

1 cup sour cream

¼ cup honey

¼ teaspoon vanilla

Beat ingredients. Spoon into a hole in cupcakes. Bake again for 5 minutes at 300 degrees. Garnish with fresh fruit.

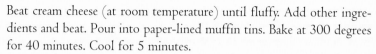

COCONUT DREAM BARS

Crust Layer:

1 stick butter, softened

⅛ teaspoon sea salt ✦ ¼ cup honey

½ teaspoon vanilla ✦ 1 cup whole wheat flour

Preheat oven to 350 degrees. Stir butter, honey, salt, and vanilla together with a fork. Add flour and stir until creamy. Pat mixture into bottom of an ungreased 8-inch square pan. Bake for 10 minutes.

While crust bakes, mix topping:

2 eggs (room temperature) ✦ 3 tablespoons honey

2 tablespoons whole wheat flour

1 rounded teaspoon baking powder ✦ ½ cup maple syrup

¼ teaspoon sea salt ✦ 1 teaspoon vanilla

Mix the above with electric mixer. Add 1 ¼ cups fine grated unsweetened coconut and ½ cup fine chopped pecans. Mix well and pour over crust. Bake 25 to 30 minutes until light golden brown. Cool for 10 minutes. While still warm, carefully cut into 24 bars.

VEGETABLE SANDWICHES

*3 types of fresh vegetables
(zucchini, carrots, and cauliflower taste good)*

1 cup celery, chopped ✦ 1 small onion, chopped

1 small bell pepper, chopped ✦ ½ cucumber, chopped

1 envelope Knox gelatin ✦ ¼ cup cold water

¼ cup boiling water ✦ ½ cup mayonnaise

1 teaspoon salt ✦ 1 loaf of your favorite bread, sliced

Drain finely chopped veggies on paper towel. Dissolve gelatin in cold water, add boiling water, and cool. Fold in mayonnaise, salt, and vegetables. Store in refrigerator until ready to make sandwiches. Spread filling on your choice of bread and cut out sandwiches with a heart-shaped cookie cutter or a round biscuit cutter.

CAROB BUTTERMILK CAKE

⅓ cup butter, softened ✦ ½ cup honey

2 eggs ✦ 1 ⅓ cups oat flour

1 teaspoon baking soda ✦ ¼ teaspoon salt

½ cup buttermilk ✦ 4 tablespoons carob powder

⅓ cup boiling water ✦ 1 teaspoon vanilla

Preheat oven to 350 degrees. Beat butter, honey, and eggs together well. Add dry ingredients alternately with buttermilk. In a small saucepan, bring water to a boil. Add carob powder, one tablespoonful at a time, stirring until blended. Add to batter along with vanilla. Beat well and pour into a buttered 8-inch square pan that has been lined with waxed paper. Bake for approximately 35 minutes. Cool and remove from pan with care. (Cake will be light and fragile.)

Cake Topping:

1 cup milk ✦ ½ cup honey ✦ 1 stick butter

3 egg yolks ✦ 1 teaspoon vanilla ✦ 1 cup pecans, chopped

1 ⅓ cups raw, unsweetened coconut

Combine milk, honey, butter, and beaten yolks in a saucepan and cook over medium heat for 12 minutes, stirring constantly. Add coconut, nuts, and vanilla. Spread over top of cake.

Note: This cake with the topping is similar to German chocolate cake—very moist.

A "Heart of a Mother" Tea

RUBY SETTLED HER DOLL INTO A TINY rocking chair displayed on the quilt on top of her dining room table. Gloria leaned her teddy bear against the bottom of the chair as Suzette added her daughter Colleen's little teapot and teacups to the table. Deciding that the scene would look cozier with one more tiny guest, Claudette snuggled a smaller doll into the rocker. A doll's parasol and some well-loved storybooks completed the sweet vignette of childhood.

At each place setting was a teacup and saucer that said, "Mother." Several of these were oversized, but that didn't bother Ruby. She reasoned that a mother's cup always looks oversized to a child. The dessert plates were children's storybook character dinner plates. All of this was placed on a caramel and white checked tablecloth. Little doll-sized hats with ribbons were tied around the off-white napkins, and small pieces of doll furniture held the place cards. All of this was for Laura, who had been summoned to Ruby's for what was mysteriously described as an urgent meeting of Sandy's Tea Society.

A becoming-more-expectant Laura walked toward Ruby's front porch in her sensible shoes.

At least she hoped she was walking! She felt like she was beginning to waddle a little, but it was so hard to see her feet that she couldn't be sure. She was curious about the reason for the meeting. Could it be that it was time to assemble the friendship quilt? She hoped not. Her quilt square was not quite ready. She knew that this gathering wasn't a baby shower—it wasn't quite time for that. Soon she would discover that this afternoon had been planned to give her confidence and encouragement about becoming a mother—and to show her that the tea society was already confident that she would be terrific in the role.

When Ruby welcomed her warmly at the front door, Laura saw the table and realized that she was there for tea. But she was a bit puzzled. "Is this a little girl tea party?" she asked, wondering where the little girls were.

"No," explained Ruby, "but it *is* a child's tea. For we are all someone's child. We want to share a mother's heart with you through the eyes of a child."

And so began a childhood remembrance of what was special about mothers, with each of

GAMES, BOOKS, AND OTHER FUN
TO BRING OUT THE LITTLE GIRL IN YOU

- Hopscotch
- Jacks
- Checkers
- *Little House* series
  by Laura Ingalls Winder
- Jump Rope
- Tag
- Pick-up Sticks
- Ring Around the Rosy
- Coloring
- Paper Dolls

- *Anne of Green Gables*
  by L. M. Montgomery
- Dress-up
- Daisy Chains
- Tree Climbing
- Playing House
- Four-square
- Roller Skates
- Swinging
- Hula Hoop
- Hide-and-Seek
- Marbles

the ladies sharing extraordinary memories from ordinary things. Laura was absolutely beaming as she tried to guess whom each toy had belonged to as they congregated around the table.

Even the menu was straight from the heart of a child. There was no fancy food here—only childhood favorites: individual custards, peanut butter and jelly sandwiches, animal crackers, small scones, and chocolate milk in the teapot. Turning the clock back to the springtime of life was fun!

Ruby invited Lillian to share her memento first. "This is my mother's purse," she said, holding out a tapestry handbag. "She called it her 'bag.' It held so many things—a handkerchief to dab dirt off my face or to dry a tear, a nickel for the ice-cream man, a comb, a small bandage, a stick of gum….It seemed like she always had whatever I needed. With her purse she was prepared for anything!"

"This book," shared Gloria, lifting a childhood storybook off the table, "will never let me forget that my mother had time for me. When I sat in her lap and she read to me, I had no idea that there was anything else in the world she could be doing."

Unfolding her mother's faded red apron, Suzette said, "When my mother put on this apron, I knew it was time for her to get busy. It was like her work uniform. This apron gave me the feeling that my mother was capable and that things were well taken care of."

Ruby pulled a small scrap of wallpaper out of her pocket. "I probably learned to love the layers of color in a pattern by staring at this wallpaper. I looked and looked at it when my mother had me stand in the corner to reconsider my behavior," she mused with a small smile. "But my times in that kitchen corner taught me that my mother meant what she said. Her consistency made me feel very secure."

Veronica opened her hand to reveal two beautiful pearl earrings. "I learned from my mother what it meant to be feminine. She has always been careful to take time to look her best. She taught me how to act like a lady and that 'pretty is as pretty does.' She still has an ageless inner beauty."

Claudette carefully held up a beautiful teacup. "As you all know, my mother taught

Ruby's Teacup

me how to have tea parties with the teacups that she left to me. Her gracious hospitality made me want to have a welcoming spirit."

"Every memory and every memento you have shared has touched my heart," Laura began, "and I feel like all of you together have just described my mother. I now realize that I *do* have a mother's heart. My mother taught it to me as she has lived it! She has always been preparing her child to be a mother. Oh, Claire!" she interrupted herself. "I'm sorry; I forgot that you have not yet told us about your mother."

"Well," said Claire, as she gently pulled the string strap of an old conical birthday party hat under her chin, "my mother found a lot of joy in surprises. She delighted in surprising us at birthdays and at Christmas and with a surprise for no reason at all. And," she continued, not able to restrain a smile, "I suspect that your mother likes surprises, too."

"Isn't that your husband coming up the walk?" asked Ruby as she pulled Laura to the window. Looking out, Laura did indeed see her husband—and he was not alone. He was bringing her mother, Mary! Laura was absolutely speechless with joy. She managed one word,

"How?" as she looked around at the others.

"In the eyes of these 'children,'" Ruby declared, "the perfect gift is a train ticket for Mother!"

⮍

Claudette, whose mother was no longer living, was feeling a little lonely by the time she arrived home from the tea party. Approaching her front door, she found a gift beside it. Eagerly she took it inside and began to tear the pretty paper off. She pried the lid off the box and lifted out a beautiful teapot with a little card tied to the handle—"The tea from this pot is steeped with love for a friend sent from above."

Friends could never take the place of her mother, but she was even more grateful right now for her mother's wisdom and love of hospitality. Her mother had known that she could not always be with her, but if she used her teacups to make friends, she would never be lonely. How could she feel alone? She had a Secret Sipper!

"Heart of a Mother"
TEA MENU

Sugar Scones
Custard Cups
Peanut Butter and Jelly Sandwiches
Animal Crackers
Chocolate Milk

SUGAR SCONES

2 cups flour

1 teaspoon baking powder

¼ cup butter ✦ 1 teaspoon vanilla

5 teaspoons sugar ✦ ⅔ cup milk

Preheat oven to 425 degrees. Dust a baking sheet with flour. Sift flour and baking powder into a mixing bowl, then stir to mix. Add butter and vanilla, then stir in sugar. Make a well in the center of the dry mixture. Add milk, mixing it in until dough is soft but not sticky. Turn out dough onto a floured surface and knead lightly. Pat dough out to 1-inch thickness. Using a round cookie cutter, cut out 12 scones. Arrange on a floured baking sheet and dust the tops of the scones with cinnamon. Bake for 12 minutes or until lightly browned. Serve with butter or jam.

CUSTARD CUPS

½ cup sugar ✦ ½ teaspoon salt ✦ ¼ teaspoon nutmeg

1 teaspoon vanilla ✦ 2 ⅔ cups milk ✦ 3 large eggs

Preheat oven to 400 degrees. Beat eggs slightly with mixer, then add in rest of ingredients and beat well. Add mix to custard cups. Put custard cups in a shallow pan containing hot water and bake for 15 minutes, then lower oven temperature to 325 degrees and finish baking for another 45 minutes. Test custard before removing to make sure it is done all the way through. To do this, insert a knife into side of filling and be sure it comes out clean. Center will be soft but will firm up later.

PEANUT BUTTER AND JELLY SANDWICHES

creamy peanut butter ✦ grape jelly

white bread

After making the peanut butter and jelly sandwiches (be sure to trim off the crusts), use animal-shaped cookie cutters to create fun shapes. Your collection of animals could be a zoo, a circus, or even Noah's ark!

A "Wishing You Blue Skies" Tea

"NO, NO! LET ME CLIMB THE LADDER," insisted Veronica.

Starting next to the chandelier over the table, she gathered the end of a long trail of white tulle and fastened it with a length of picture framing wire to the chandelier. About a yard farther down the length of the tulle, she gathered it again and fastened it with another piece of wire. After she had stuffed it with a little white tissue paper to make a "pouf," Laura handed her a generous glob of sticky putty to hold the "cloud" to the ceiling.

Veronica repeated the poufs of clouds across the ceiling until she got to the corner of the room, where she trimmed off any leftover length of fabric. Starting again at the chandelier, she worked outward to another corner. When all four corners were done, Veronica hopped down and the two ladies admired their "canopy of clouds." The effect was not of storm clouds but puffy, sunny-day clouds.

Together Veronica and Laura had prepared a "Wishing You Blue Skies" tea for their friend Anna who was weathering some of life's cloudy days. In only one month, all three of her children had had chicken pox—not in unison, but consecutively—her basement had flooded twice, and her husband had been temporarily laid off from his job. It was time to get Anna out of her house and to give her some encouragement!

Laura had set the table with her own white dessert plates and borrowed Suzette's blue and white china teacups and saucers. On the white serving plates were white paper doilies under pineapple delight sandwiches, "clouds" with blue skies, lemon shortbread squares, and scones with tropical fruit. White napkins edged in white eyelet lace were tied with a yellow grosgrain ribbon with a pair of inexpensive white sunglasses tucked in.

Now that everything was ready, the ladies hurried to change into their tea party clothes. Everyone was planning to wear blue and white today!

Anna arrived at the same time as the other ladies, offering Laura a hostess gift of a warm loaf of banana nut bread wrapped in a pretty new tea towel and tied with a ribbon. Laura thanked her for such a thoughtful gift and hurried to add it to the tea table while Anna became acquainted with the ladies she didn't know.

Anna was amazed at the generosity of

SUNNY SKIES ABOVE

The tea society decorated everything for this party
in blue and white with a few sunny yellow accents.

❧ *Suzette loaned her hand-painted blue dining room chairs for the occasion.*

❧ *The table was draped in a long blue cloth.*

❧ *With safety pins, Laura and Veronica fashioned big, puffy bows
of more white tulle to the outside edge of the table, leaving "swoops"
of tulle in between each bow.*

❧ *Every chair back was dressed with a big
white tulle bow with long tails.*

❧ *In the center of the table, standing in a blue
and white china pitcher, was a big bouquet
of yellow roses mixed with blue hydrangeas.*

Laura's Teacup

spirit that had created such a lovely tea just for her. As soon as all the ladies were seated around the table, Laura offered a simple grace of thanksgiving for blue skies above all our storms and then began to pour the lemon herbal tea.

"Anna," Lillian ventured sympathetically, "I understand that you have had one thing right after the other at your house."

"Yes," Anna said dryly, with a little smile. "They say when it rains, it pours. But I didn't know it was going to be in my basement!"

One by one, the ladies shared their own experiences of sick children, job losses, even a house fire, with each one sharing how every bad thing that had happened had ultimately worked for good. But they understood how discouraging it could feel to be in the midst of trouble.

Soon they were almost competing to see who had had the worst experiences with lack of money, home repairs, and calamities. They were absolutely joyful over the things that they had survived and were sure that those events had made them stronger. Seeing that these friends could now treasure their troubles gave Anna the

to climb and then make sunbeams around her face with her fingers before Suzette began to wave her hand. "Climb Up Sunshine Mountain!"

"You're right!" said Gloria with relief.

What fun they had together! A "sunny" afternoon was just the break that Anna needed. She was amazed. In spite of everything she had learned in science class, today she had found that the sun does indeed shine under the clouds!

Before it was time to say good-bye, Laura presented Anna with a pretty blue parasol on behalf of the entire tea society. On it Laura had written encouraging words and verses of faith, hope, and love. The tag on the handle read:

Until once again you have sunny skies above,
Walk under your umbrella of faith, hope, and love.

Anna was so grateful for their thoughtfulness. She was wavering between tears and words of thanks when some of the putty on the ceiling began to give way and the fabric clouds started falling. "See?" quipped Ruby. "We told you the clouds would disappear!"

hope that someday soon she would laugh about a tight budget and three cases of chicken pox. More than anything, they wanted her to see that she was in the midst of a rainy season, not a rainy life.

For a lighthearted touch, Laura had asked Ruby to provide the entertainment for them. "My mother said it wasn't polite to sing at the table, so I decided that we would pantomime some songs. Each of you can choose a song for us to guess, but it must be about sunshine or blue skies."

Claudette paused for a moment, then began to gesture upward and then back to herself—smiling broadly all the time.

"I get it! I get it!" said Gloria excitedly. "Blue Skies Smiling at Me!"

"Okay," said Ruby, "you're next." It took quite a bit of Gloria's using her arms to pretend

Laura's Teapot

"Wishing You Blue Skies"

TEA MENU

Lemon Shortbread Squares
Pineapple Delight Sandwiches
Clouds with Blue Skies
Scones with Tropical Fruit
Lemon Herbal Tea

LEMON SHORTBREAD SQUARES

1 ¼ cup flour ✦ ½ cup powdered sugar

½ teaspoon vanilla ✦ ½ teaspoon lemon juice (freshly squeezed or bottled)

½ cup plus 2 tablespoons butter (real) at room temperature

½ cup almonds, finely chopped

Preheat oven to 325 degrees. In a large bowl, combine all ingredients, except almonds. Beat until dough is smooth and comes away clean from the sides of the bowl, then gather into a ball (like bread dough). With well-floured fingers, press dough evenly over the bottom of a 9-inch square ungreased baking dish. (Both metal and glass work fine.) Sprinkle almonds on top and press gently into the dough. Using a sharp knife, score into 16 small squares and prick each square twice with a fork. Bake until dough is barely colored and almonds are lightly toasted (about 20 minutes). Let cool for 5 minutes, then cut squares all the way through. Cool completely in pan. Store shortbread squares in an airtight container for up to 2 weeks.

for 1 hour. (Keep a close eye on these while baking; they should not turn brown.) Turn oven off and let the cups sit in the oven 2 hours longer. Remove and slowly peel cups from paper. They will now be ready to fill with blueberries or any fruit of your choice and sprinkle with powdered sugar.

SCONES WITH TROPICAL FRUIT

2 cups flour ✦ *½ cup sugar*

2 teaspoons baking powder ✦ *¼ teaspoon salt*

⅓ cup butter, chilled ✦ *½ cup half-and-half*

1 large egg ✦ *1 teaspoon vanilla*

½ cup dried tropical fruit mix, minced

In a large bowl, stir together flour, sugar, baking powder, and salt. Cut the butter into small pieces on top of the flour mixture. Using a pastry blender or two knives, cut the butter into the flour mixture until it resembles coarse crumbs. In a separate bowl, mix together the half-and-half, egg, vanilla, and dried tropical fruit. Add to the flour mixture. The dough will be very moist. (With scones, always take care not to over-handle the dough.) With floured hands, turn dough out onto a lightly floured cookie sheet and shape into an 8- or 9-inch circle. With a serrated knife, cut into 8 wedges. Bake for 15 minutes at 425 degrees. Remove from oven and cool on a wire rack for 10 minutes. Serve warm.

IGHT
S

erature)

d out)

sliced

heat,

s together. a layer of mixture. Top with bread slice. Cut off crusts and cut diagonally into triangles. Chill.

CLOUDS WITH BLUE SKIES

2 egg whites ✦ *¼ teaspoon cream of tartar*

½ cup sugar ✦ *1 teaspoon vinegar*

¼ teaspoon almond or vanilla extract

Preheat oven to 250 degrees. Beat egg whites, cream of tartar, and vinegar until soft peaks form. Blend in sugar (very slowly) until completely dissolved and stiff peaks form. Blend in extract flavoring. Place a sheet of heavy brown paper or "baker's paper" on a cookie sheet. Take meringue and drop in 3-inch circles on paper. Gently "hollow" out the center of each meringue. Bake in a 250-degree oven

A "Loving Hands" Tea

"THIS IS WHAT I HAVE." IN A SWEEPING gesture Veronica pointed to all of the favorite things in her living room—pillows, chairs, lamps, pictures, and rugs. The tea society studied the grouping carefully. Veronica had asked them to give her some decorating ideas. Although she moved often, she liked to make her nest her own in every place she lived. It was a challenge. She never knew what color carpet, paint, or wallpaper she would find.

Through repeated packing and moving and discarding superfluous things, she had refined her taste and surrounded herself with the things she really liked. But now she had to make a big decision. Her sofa badly needed covering, and she had no curtains. How could she tie all these special things together? What would look nice and homey here as well as in unknown places where she might someday live?

Claudette picked up a lovely black needlepoint pillow with a floral design and walked over to a table draped with a hand-crocheted cloth.

She noticed that on several tables, Veronica had doilies or dresser scarves with flower baskets embroidered on them. "I collect them wherever I go," explained Veronica. "There must be an endless variety, for I never seem to find a duplicate. But they are a continual theme for me, and they help make every place I live seem like home."

"Could I please borrow some of these handmade things for our 'Loving Hands' tea? With the laces and vintage fashions that I have and some of the handmade things Suzette has, we can create a lovely tribute to these kinds of handwork."

"Oh, please do," replied Veronica. "Take them and use them anyway you like for your tea."

"I'll be very careful with them."

"Don't worry—I know how to clean them," Veronica assured her.

"Toile."

"Excuse me?" came a chorus.

"Toile," Ruby repeated decidedly.

"What is toile?" asked Veronica.

"Oh!" began Claudette excitedly. "Toile is a fabric—or wallpaper—pattern, traditionally in a one- or two-color drawing. One or several drawings tell a story and are repeated to make the decorative pattern. I believe its origins are French, and its beauty—well, it's timeless."

"Exactly," said Ruby, "and toile is a pattern that blends nicely with stripes, checks, or florals. It can tie everything you have together—your floral pillows, your needlepoint pillows, your striped chair, and your hooked rug! A black and off-white toile with black piping would be a perfect covering for your sofa. And you could use it anywhere, though I wish it would always be here."

Veronica was already getting excited! Changing just her sofa wasn't too extreme or too expensive. "But what about the windows?"

"My mother and I will make you simple swags out of the toile with a bow on each side for your windows. It will be a housewarming present!" volunteered Suzette.

⌒

The day Veronica's newly dressed sofa arrived, Suzette and Ruby showed up at her house with a hammer and some small nails. In no time, they had tacked up the new swags. They stepped back and with a "ta-da!" let Veronica appraise the effect.

Claire's Hat

"Beautiful! Absolutely beautiful!" enthused Veronica. "My living room looks so fresh and charming!"

"It is a look that can travel," Suzette added, "but I hope it doesn't."

"I also hope that it never has to travel. Everything is just perfect here. And while we're using the hammer and nails, I have a new plate that I would like to hang on the wall." Veronica handed a vintage red and white transfer plate to Ruby.

"It's lovely; the pattern reminds me of toile. Where did you find it?" asked Ruby.

"It just came in the mail yesterday. I remember telling someone how much I wanted one, but I can't remember who I told!"

"You must have mentioned it to a Secret Sipper," Suzette said knowingly. Neither she nor Ruby admitted a thing. All of Sandy's Tea Society had adapted very well to the clandestine lives of Secret Sippers.

The other newest member of the

Claire's Shoe

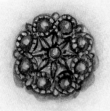

HANDS, HEARTS,
AND HEIRLOOMS

Claudette had great fun decorating for the "Loving Hands" tea!

❧ She tucked an old crocheted bedspread around the cushions of her sofa and used it as a slipcover.

❧ Above her sofa, where a pair of paintings usually hung, she displayed two antique shirtwaists side by side on satin-covered hangers.

❧ She draped lacy doilies over lampshades.

❧ She opened the lid of her grandmother's treadle sewing machine. On top of it she placed vintage sewing items with notions, old buttons, and strips of lace spilling out of the drawers.

❧ She decorated the coffee table with a basket of yarn balls and two antique knitting needles.

❧ She placed candles in large, antique wooden thread spools of random heights.

❧ On one wall she hung an old sampler stitched long ago by a little girl.

tea society, Claire, had fit into the tea society as comfortably as Veronica had. Everyone loved her and used her as a resource for all the domestic things they didn't know how to do. Along with her official welcoming tea party, Claudette wanted to introduce her to some silver tea ladies her own age. She knew other ladies who also had skills for things her generation had neither the time nor the training for. She wanted the tea to honor them as well as Claire and acknowledge how special they were with a salute to handmade things.

When the tea society ladies and the special guests arrived at Claudette's "Loving Hands" tea, they found she had transformed her dining room and living room with handmade items. All of the silver tea ladies felt honored to be appreciated in such a lovely way, but especially Claire. She had embroidered a pretty little pillow as a hostess gift for Claudette in anticipation of this party. On it was the perfect message: "May your home always be too small for all your friends." Claudette, so delighted with her new pillow that she continued to clutch it, introduced each silver tea lady to Claire and to each member of the tea society before they were seated at the table.

In the dining room, they found an old dress form wearing a handmade, lace Victorian day dress standing watch over the tea goodies and the beautiful table. The crocheted tablecloth that Claudette had borrowed covered the table. At each place was one of Veronica's dresser scarves embroidered with a flower basket as a place mat. Using two inexpensive clear glass plates of exactly the same size and shape, Claudette had sandwiched a small crocheted doily between them for the dessert plate. Nothing could be closer to eating right off a lacy doily! The teacups and saucers were an assortment of pastel colors of Depression glass. What a pretty and feminine table! And for each guest, Claudette had embroidered a monogram on a white cotton napkin as a favor to take home.

Claudette's Teacup

Candles were glowing in an assortment of pastel-colored glass candlesticks and a pink Depression glass fan vase held white hydrangea blooms. Pastel glass cookie and cake plates displayed the assortment of treats Claudette had so carefully prepared from recipes that several of the silver tea ladies had shared with her.

As Claudette poured the peach tea from her beautiful new friendship teapot, she examined the face of each lady in the tea society, hoping for a clue to the giver. But they were inscrutable! Conversation around the table was as warm as the tea. The younger tea society ladies found they had

much in common with the older silver tea ladies, all of whom wanted Claire as a new friend. Her social calendar was going to be full, indeed.

Each of the silver tea ladies had been invited to bring something she had made to share with the rest of the group. After they had enjoyed their time at the tea table, they gathered in the living room. Explaining the technique for each kind of handwork and displaying the proper needles or tools, each lady showcased her work. Everyone was especially amazed at Helen's bobbin lace. What beautiful, intricate work emerged from the interchange of the hand-carved bobbins of thread on the pillow!

"Miss Elizabeth," Gloria asked one of the older ladies respectfully, "what do you receive from the time you put into your handwork?"

"Oh, there is such joy for me in creating something beautiful. How would you other ladies describe creativity in your lives?"

"Contentment."

"Satisfaction."

"Accomplishment."

"The pleasure of giving."

"I knew that once you met these ladies," Claudette began with a twinkle in her eye, "you would want that same satisfaction of making something with your own hands. So, today I have enough looms and knit loops for us all to weave a pot holder while we visit."

"What fun!" cheered Laura.

"I want all of the red loops," said Ruby playfully.

"No fair!" Lillian bantered back with a smile.

"Who will get the pot holders?" questioned Ruby as she offered the bag of loops to one of their guests.

"Every child knows," replied Suzette, "that a pot holder is a gift for Mama. But I don't think mine will mind if we give them all to Gloria. She'll need them right away as she learns to cook for her new husband."

"What a good idea," agreed Claire. "We'll craft her a wonderful collection."

⁓

The following week, Claire visited everyone in Sandy's Tea Society, helping each of them finish their appliqued quilt squares and collecting them as she went. After she had gathered the last one from Gloria, she placed them all in her sewing basket. What was that? Her eyes caught a glint of light. There in the basket was a gleaming little silver shoe pincushion! A Secret Sipper had struck again. Or was it a Silver Secret Sipper?

"Loving Hands"
TEA MENU

English Dates
Irish Soda Bread
Pecan Wafers
Sour Cream Drops
Hot Chicken Salad
Peach Tea

ENGLISH DATES

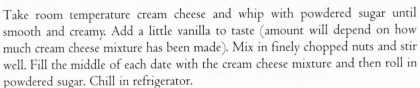

large dates, pitted

cream cheese

powdered sugar

vanilla

walnuts, pecans,
or almonds, finely chopped

Take room temperature cream cheese and whip with powdered sugar until smooth and creamy. Add a little vanilla to taste (amount will depend on how much cream cheese mixture has been made). Mix in finely chopped nuts and stir well. Fill the middle of each date with the cream cheese mixture and then roll in powdered sugar. Chill in refrigerator.

IRISH SODA BREAD

4 cups flour ✦ 3 tablespoons sugar

1 tablespoon baking powder ✦ 1 teaspoon salt

¾ teaspoon baking soda ✦ ¾ stick butter (real)

1 cup raisins ✦ 2 eggs, beaten ✦ 1 ½ cups buttermilk

Grease a 2-quart round casserole. In a large bowl, mix flour, sugar, baking powder, and salt together with a fork. With a pastry blender or fork, cut in butter until mixture resembles coarse crumbs. Stir in raisins. Preheat oven to 350 degrees. In a small bowl, beat eggs slightly. Remove 1 tablespoonful of beaten egg and reserve it for later. Stir remaining egg and buttermilk into flour mixture just until flour is moistened. Dough will be sticky. Turn dough onto a floured surface. With floured hands, knead dough about 10 strokes to mix thoroughly. Use ample amount of flour. Shape dough into a ball and place in a greased casserole dish. With a sharp knife, cut a 4-inch cross about 1/4-inch deep into the center of the dough ball. Brush dough with the reserved egg for a shiny surface after baking. Bake in a 350-degree oven for 60-70 minutes or until a toothpick inserted in the center comes out clean. Cool on a wire rack for 10 minutes, then remove bread from casserole dish and cool on the rack for an additional 30 minutes (or longer for easier slicing).

PECAN WAFERS

3 egg whites ✦ ⅛ teaspoon salt

1 ¼ cup brown sugar (either dark or light)

3 tablespoons melted butter (real)

1 teaspoon vanilla ✦ 2 tablespoons flour

1 cup pecans, finely chopped

Preheat oven to 350 degrees. Cover cookie sheets with aluminum foil (the heavier the better); grease well with vegetable shortening. Set aside. Beat egg whites and salt in a medium-sized heavy bowl until stiff. Set aside. In separate bowl, combine sugar, butter, vanilla, and flour. Fold the sugar mixture into the egg whites, just until uniformly combined. Gently fold in pecans. On prepared cookie sheets, drop slightly rounded teaspoonfuls of dough 3 inches apart. Bake in a preheated 350-degree oven for 12-15 minutes, just until centers and edges are evenly cooked. Cool on foil. Store in airtight containers.

SOUR CREAM DROPS

½ cup shortening ✦ 1 ½ cups sugar

2 eggs ✦ 1 cup sour cream ✦ 1 teaspoon vanilla

2 ¾ cups flour ✦ ½ teaspoon baking soda

½ teaspoon baking powder ✦ ½ teaspoon salt

Preheat oven to 325-350 degrees (depending on how hot your oven runs). Grease cookie sheets with shortening. Cream together shortening and sugar. Beat in eggs. Fold in sour cream and vanilla just until well blended. Sift together the flour, soda, baking powder, and salt in a separate bowl. Gently stir flour mixture in with the previous ingredients until well mixed, but do not over-mix, as this will make the dough tough. Drop by rounded teaspoonfuls onto greased cookie sheets. Bake for 8-10 minutes until set and not "doughy" in the middle any longer. Cool on cookie sheets for a couple of minutes, then gently move to cooling racks and cool completely. Keep tightly covered.

HOT CHICKEN SALAD

2 cups chicken breast, cooked and diced

2 cups celery, diced ✦ ¾ cup mayonnaise

½ cup toasted almonds

¼ cup onion, finely chopped

2 tablespoons lemon juice ✦ ½ teaspoon salt

1 cup cheddar cheese, grated

1 cup potato chips, crushed

Mix together the first seven ingredients and place in a 2-quart casserole dish. Top with cheese and potato chips. Bake in a 350-degree oven for 30 minutes.

Teatime at Sandy's

COME ON IN! EVERYTHING IS READY for today's friendship tea. Not only have I kept the identity of the Secret Sippers a secret, I've been careful to keep Claire's secret for today—and Veronica's too. Are you as eager as the ladies in Sandy's Tea Society to name the Secret Sippers? I can hardly wait to see Laura, Claudette, Lillian, Suzette, Ruby, Gloria, Veronica, and Claire! I want to ask them a question.

I can see through the window that I won't have long to wait! All of them are arriving early, and they're all wearing their aprons. Let's receive each of them with a genuine fondness amidst this air of excitement and anticipation.

As I begin serving very simple tea with scones and jam, chicken salad sandwiches, and Sandy's Tea Society cake, I can wait no longer to see if they have enjoyed serving others in love with their "heart and hands" teas as much as they have enjoyed serving each other.

"Oh, even more!" answers Lillian when I ask the question. "We have all been enriched by those we have tried to serve. I think we would all agree that our own friendships have become even more golden as we have added new friends to our lives."

"Love is like tea," adds Claudette. "It's meant to be poured out."

"Well, if you will join me in the next

room," I pause, letting the suspense build, "Claire has a surprise for you."

Claire stands up and holds the door open. When the ladies all have entered the room, she turns on the light. The room is filled with gasps of delight, for there in the middle is a small quilting frame surrounded by chairs. And on the frame is their friendship quilt! Not only has Claire pieced together the squares the ladies have made describing their tea parties, she has also created a quilt square with a teacup for each of them. They all blink back tears as they thank her for this labor of love and sit down around the quilt, eager to learn how to finish it.

Patiently, Claire shows all of us how to actually "quilt," attaching the pieced quilt top through the batting to the backing with tiny, even stitches. We are glad it will take several sessions to finish. These quilting bees will give us another excuse to visit!

Stitching away, with a needle prick here and a needle prick there (ouch!), we talk about our "hearts and hands" tea parties and how it is more blessed to give than to receive. Remembering that we have not yet revealed the identities of the Secret Sippers, Laura remarks, "It is much easier to give than to receive, especially when you don't know who to thank. You just have to receive without being able to say 'thank you' or do anything in return."

Individually the ladies begin to share the multiple acts of kindness that had been done for them, still not knowing the givers.

"I want to know who my Secret Sipper is who has been so kind to me, but I'd rather remain anonymous to the one I've been a Secret Sipper to," says Ruby thoughtfully.

"Would you like to vote and decide if you really want to reveal your identities?" I ask.

"Yes!" they agree.

"How many would like to know who your Secret Sipper is?" Everyone raises her hand. "It looks unanimous, but how many want their own identity as a Secret Sipper to remain a secret?" They all raise their hands again.

"I have an idea," I say. "Why don't we keep our identities a secret for the joy of doing and giving without being thanked?"

We all agree heartily and decide to change Secret Sippers at the next tea and do it all over again.

Then Laura speaks up. "I won't reveal who I have been a Secret Sipper to, but I know

what I did for her, and I didn't do all of the wonderful acts of kindness she received." The others chime in—except for Veronica. They had noticed the same mysterious thing when the kindnesses were shared. Their Secret Sippers received more than they gave.

I look over at Veronica who, with a blush, confesses, "You were all so sweet to welcome and include me that I adopted *all* of you as my Secret Sippers."

"But we wanted you as our friend," assures Claudette. "You didn't have to do so very much for all of us."

"Oh, but I wanted to," protests Veronica, "and I'm so glad that I did. I just found out that my husband's work is moving him again, and I have to leave in six more weeks."

This is Veronica's sad surprise. The ladies in Sandy's Tea Society look at each other with eyes bright with tears. I know they are all thinking the same thing, but it is Lillian who speaks it. "Veronica, we want to give our friendship quilt to you when it's finished. You truly have the heart of Sandy's

Tea Society. You will be our first ambassador to another city!"

Veronica brightens at this expression of the depth of their friendship—and at the prospect of beginning a chapter of Sandy's Tea Society in a new place. "Perhaps I could start it with a 'Come and Meet Your New Neighbor' tea. Wherever I am, I will continue your mission to join kindred hearts with a cup of friendship."

Ruby had brought Veronica to us as a symbol of what our tea society is all about, a new silver friend. But in a very short time she has become a golden friend, indeed.

SANDY'S TEA SOCIETY CAKE

2 cups sugar ✦ 2 cups flour

1 teaspoon baking soda ✦ 2 teaspoons cinnamon

1 teaspoon instant coffee granules

2 sticks margarine ✦ 4 tsps cocoa ✦ 1 cup water

½ cup buttermilk ✦ 2 eggs ✦ 1 teaspoon vanilla

1 teaspoon orange extract

Sift together flour, sugar, baking soda, cinnamon, and coffee. Set aside. In a saucepan, melt margarine. Add cocoa and water and bring to a boil. Pour over flour mixture. Quickly add buttermilk, eggs, vanilla, and orange extract. Mix well. Pour into a greased and floured 9 x 13 baking dish. Bake at 400 degrees for 20 minutes or when top springs back when touched.

ICING

1 stick margarine, melted

4 tbsps cocoa ✦ 6 tbsps buttermilk

1 tbsp vanilla ✦ 1 tsp instant coffee granules

1 tsp orange extract ✦ 1 box powdered sugar

1 cup chopped pecans or slivered almonds

In a large saucepan, combine margarine, cocoa, and buttermilk. Bring to a boil. Stir in vanilla, coffee, and orange extract. Reduce heat. Add powdered sugar and nuts. Mix well. Pour over cake.

Postscript

WOULD YOU LIKE TO BE an ambassador of Sandy's Tea Society in your neighborhood? You can do that by developing true friendships with acts of kindness around a warm cup of tea. Your chapter can also serve others by pouring out love in "hands and hearts" teas.

If you would like to join Sandy's Tea Society, please contact us at the address below. You can also find additional tea party ideas and other kindred hearts sharing their own special tea parties on our website, also noted below.

Finally, if you are wondering how Ruby, Gloria, Suzette, Lillian, and Claudette met and developed their friendships, we invite you to read *Sandy's Tea Society: Delighting in Friendships Steeped in Love.* You will be treated to a touch of heartfelt hospitality and the exciting opportunity to deepen your own friendships.

SANDY'S TEA SOCIETY
P.O. Box 85
Powder Springs, GA
30127-0085

Or we invite you to join us
on the Internet at:

www.sandysteasociety.com

There is a tea party waiting there for you!